508
HAE

Haegele, Katie.

Cool careers without
college for nature
lovers.

$30.60

34880030018852

DATE			

COOL CAREERS WITHOUT COLLEGE FOR

NATURE

LOVERS

COOL CAREERS WITHOUT COLLEGE FOR NATURE LOVERS

KATIE HAEGELE

The Rosen Publishing Group, Inc.
New York

Published in 2002 by The Rosen Publishing Group, Inc.
29 East 21st Street, New York, NY 10010

Library of Congress Cataloging-in-Publication Data

Haegele, Katie.
Cool careers without college for nature lovers / Katie Haegele.
p. cm. — (Cool careers without college)
Includes bibliographical references (p.).
Summary: Profiles the characteristics of and qualifications needed for twelve jobs that involve working with nature.
ISBN 0-8239-3504-3 (lib. binding)
1. Natural history—Vocational guidance—Juvenile literature.
[1. Natural history—Vocational guidance. 2. Vocational guidance.]
I. Title. II. Series.
QH49 .H34 2001
508'.023—dc21

2001003911

Manufactured in the United States of America

CONTENTS

INTRODUCTION

When you hear the word "career," do you think of large, monolithic corporations, featureless glass office buildings, and sterile, claustrophobic office cubicles? Do you imagine hours of photocopying, shuffling papers, and staring bleary-eyed at a computer monitor under bleak florescent lights? What if you were offered the opportunity to work on a ship that sailed the sea in search of great big whales or voyaged to remote, unspoiled areas of the world, such as the Arctic Circle?

What if you could be living and working in a national park, leading a cattle drive on horseback, or transforming an abandoned city lot into a beautiful green space?

For some lucky people, work means being outside every day, interacting closely with the environment, and pursuing a passion for nature. Many cool careers exist for nature lovers, and many of them do not require a college degree in order to get your foot in the door. In this book, you will be introduced to many jobs that will allow you to earn money in the great outdoors. All of these jobs emphasize hands-on experience as much as formal academic training. So if you have a passion for the work and are willing to initially perform "grunt" duties for low pay, you should find opportunities for advancement before long. If advancement is dependent upon academic training, many of these jobs provide the necessary courses and programs. In addition, courses taken at a community college or technical school can also often satisfy job requirements.

Deriving a sense of satisfaction and fulfillment from a job is often a question of pursuing your interests. If you wish to spend every workday in nature, do not assume that such a desire is an idle daydream. You can make a living from your passion for the outdoors, and this book will show you how to go about finding a job that benefits both you and the environment.

1

CHRISTMAS TREE FARMER

Christmas may come only once a year, but Christmas tree farmers are busy on every one of the 364 other days, too! In fact, it is during the summer that tree farmers work the most and earn the most money. If you can combine a knack for cultivating trees with good communication skills and some business sense, you could build your own business—and a very lucrative career.

A farmer tends to Christmas trees on her tree farm in Texas.

Description

The initial investment needed to start a tree farm can be large because it takes from six to twelve years for the first crop to grow to selling size. One of the reasons Christmas tree farming can be profitable, however, is that fir and pine trees can flourish on marginal or less fertile land. This type of land is far less expensive to purchase.

Christmas tree farmers need to be knowledgeable about trees in general and popular Christmas tree species in particular. One crop of trees requires a year's work, and the yield is not always high. Approximately 2,000 trees are planted per acre on the average tree farm, but only 750 to 1,500 trees survive to harvest. The good news is that an average of 33 million trees are sold each year, resulting in annual sales of between $360 and $540 million.

A typical Christmas tree farm's cycle begins in March and April, when farmers plant a crop of new trees with seedlings that are grown from seed in beds or greenhouses. A seedling is a small tree that is usually between eight and sixteen inches tall. The planting is done either by hand or with the help of a planting machine that is mounted on a tractor.

In the spring and summer, farmers must pay close attention to the upkeep of the grounds where their trees grow. Weeds and overgrown grass, which compete with the trees for space and water, can damage the undersides of the trees, making them less attractive and harder to sell. Fire prevention is another reason for being diligent about keeping grass and weeds cut down. The grass between the trees must be mowed and the weeds controlled by covering them with mulch. An absence of grass and weeds will also keep away mice, which often kill trees by eating their bark. Insects and disease can also become a problem at this time of the year. Pruning, or the removal of infested or diseased

A customer buys a Christmas tree from a tree lot in Jacksonville, Florida.

trees, can help control the problem and prevent it from spreading to other trees in the crop.

During the summer months, the young trees are shaped through pruning. The cone shape and dense foliage growth that customers look for when choosing a tree is not natural. Pruning prevents the trees from growing too tall and also encourages them to branch more quickly, creating a full, bushy appearance.

Fall represents the busiest time of year for Christmas tree farmers. By October, the trees can be harvested and shipped. Some farmers allow families to choose and cut their own trees. Other farmers harvest the trees themselves and gather the cut trees together, selling them in an open area near the farm's entrance. Still others harvest the trees and ship them to city vendors. Before a tree is shipped, it must be shaken out and baled using a machine that presses the tree's branches together against the trunk, holding them in place with twine or plastic netting. This protects the tree from damage to its branches and makes it easier to handle when loading and unloading. In addition, some farmers dig up smaller trees and place them in pots, selling them to families who want a living tree that they can plant in their yard after Christmas. However the farmers choose to harvest and sell them, the trees must be ready for the early-bird buyers by the day after Thanksgiving.

Tree farmers can take some time off for the holidays, but right after Christmas, their work begins again. February and March are when the trees are culled, which means the "Charlie Brown" trees that will not be easy to sell are removed. The winter months are also devoted to equipment repair and property maintenance.

Education/Training

You do not need to get a special degree to learn how to cultivate and sell Christmas trees. Business skills are essential

Fun Facts

From the National Christmas Tree Association

- There are approximately 35 million real Christmas trees sold in North America every year.
- For every real Christmas tree harvested, two or three seedlings are planted in its place the following spring. In the spring of 2000, over 70 million Christmas tree seedlings were planted.
- There are about one million acres in production for growing Christmas trees. Each acre provides the daily oxygen requirements for eighteen people. Trees also act as natural air filters, removing up to thirteen tons of airborne pollutants per acre per year.
- There are about 15,000 Christmas tree growers in North America, and over 100,000 people are employed full- or part-time in the industry. Christmas trees are grown in all fifty states.
- The top Christmas tree producing states are Oregon, North Carolina, Pennsylvania, Michigan, Washington, California, and Wisconsin.
- The top selling Christmas trees are balsam fir, Douglas fir, Fraser fir, Scotch pine, Virginia pine, and white pine.

- It can take as long as fifteen years to grow a tree of suitable height for selling (about six feet), but the average growing time is seven years.

but can be learned through experience. According to the New Hampshire Christmas Tree Promotion Board, many tree farms in New Hampshire have their own education programs. Working at a nursery or farm will give you some background. Your best bet is to contact one of the state chapters of the National Christmas Tree Association to request more information and find out about joining. The NCTA will help you get in touch with a farmer who can answer your questions.

Profile

Bruce Niedermeier, Christmas tree farmer

Grew up in Milwaukee, Wisconsin

Eagle Boy Scout

Active in 4-H

Worked in a corporate job for four years and then bought a tree farm from his father, who had begun tree farming as a postretirement project.

WHAT'S A NORMAL DAY LIKE FOR YOU?

This is a really great job! I left the corporate world to do this. It's especially fun because it has an annual cycle. There's so much to do, but I have winters off. Plus, part of my farm is dedicated to "choose and cut"—this is the really good part. I get to meet every customer. Often, we end up having great conversations, and I meet interesting people whom I never would have otherwise encountered.

HOW DO CHRISTMAS TREES GET SO PERFECT LOOKING?

We shape the trees with knives. Normally, most trees grow a lot on the top and bottom, and the sides have no growth. We bring the top down to a set height, and this determines how dense or loose the tree is. From here, we use knives to shape the trees like cones. Consumers like perfect trees.

ANY ADVICE FOR PEOPLE WHO WANT TO OPEN A CHRISTMAS TREE FARM?

I think people have to get in touch with themselves to know what makes them happy, even if it's not what friends and family say. Tree growers are the nicest people I've ever worked with, so very nice and giving.

FOR MORE INFORMATION

ASSOCIATIONS

Balsam Fir Christmas Tree Growers of Canada
Web site: http://www.evergreenbalsam.ns.ca

Canadian Christmas Tree Growers
Web site: http://www.christmastree.net/home_eng.htm

Christmas Tree Farm Network
Web site: http://www.christmas-tree.com

National Christmas Tree Association
Web site: http://www.christree.org

Pennsylvania Christmas Tree Growers Association
Web site: http://www.christmastrees.org

WEB SITES

California Christmas Tree Association Research Library
http://www.cachristmas.com/research.htm
The following is a listing of articles that are contained in the California Christmas Tree Association Research Library.

M-8 "Christmas Tree Harvesting & Marketing for Pac. N.W. Growers." Douglass, Bernard, 1971, 20 pp.

L-2 "Ten Common Questions About Forest Tree Planting." Passof, Peter, et al., 1983, 4 pp.

L-3 "Successful Christmas Tree Planting." Adams, David, 1981, 3 pp.

L-4 "Plant Your Trees Right." Pitkin, Frank, 1982, 5 pp.

L-10 "Seedling Care and Handling." Oregon State University Ext., 1982, 4 pp.

S-2 "The Six Characteristics of Top-Grade Douglas-fir and How to Obtain Them." Douglass, Bernard, 1982, 3 pp.

S-40 "Shaping and Shearing Christmas Trees." Farrand, Edward, 1979, 2 pp.

Christmas Tree Farms
http://ok.essortment.com/christmastree_rezn.htm
An interesting article about the tradition of Christmas tree growing.

Christmas Tree Production Overview
http://hammock.iafs.ufl.edu

Economics of Growing an Acre of White Pines
http://www.ext.vt.edu/pubs/forestry/420-081/420-081.html

50 Careers in Trees
http://www.urbanforest.org/career6.html

Growing Christmas Trees in Illinois
http://www.ag.uiuc.edu/~vista/html_pubs/xmas/xmas.html
Extensive information packet, available free online.

Growing Christmas Trees in Newfoundland and Labrador
http://www.gov.nf.ca/agric/crops/GrowTrees.htm
Info on the business of tree farming, provided by the Canadian government.

Species for Christmas Tree Planting in Virginia
http://www.ext.vt.edu/pubs/forestry/420-082/420-082.html

BOOKS

Arnold, J. E. M., and Peter A. Dewees, eds. *Tree Management in Farmer Strategies*. New York: Oxford University Press, 1995.

Hilts, Steward, and Peter Mitchell. *The Woodlot Management Handbook*. Willowdale, ON: Firefly Books, 1999.

Johnson, Dave. *The Good Woodcutter's Guide: Chain Saws, Woodlots, and Portable Sawmills*. White River Junction, VT: Chelsea Green Publishing Co., 1998.

Lee, Andrew W. *Backyard Market Gardening*. Buena Vista, VA: Good Earth Publications, 1995.

Macher, Ron, and Howard W. Kerr Jr. *Making Your Small Farm Profitable*. North Adams, MA: Storey Books, 1999.

McEvoy, Thomas J. *Using Fertilizers in the Culture of Christmas Trees*. New York: Paragon, 1992.

MULTIMEDIA

Morrill Digital Library: Christmas Trees
Web site: http://web.aces.uiuc.edu/aim/ExtensionArticles/extart.forestry.christree.htm
Download a video on shearing and culturing Christmas trees.

Slide show: Insect Pests of Christmas trees
Web site: http://www.ext.vt.edu/departments/entomology/christmas

2

COMMERCIAL FISHER

Working as a commercial fisher is not always easy. The work can be physically demanding, and it often takes place in remote locations and harsh weather conditions. This job choice has some definite perks, however, such as a very independent life spent on the open sea in some of the most beautiful and unspoiled places in the world.

Description

Commercial fishers need to go where the fish are. Seasonal as well as year-round jobs are available in parts of Washington, Alaska, Florida, New England, Canada, Mexico, and Ireland—wherever there is port access to freshwater or saltwater fish and it is permissible to catch and sell seafood.

Commercial fishers catch fish and other marine life (such as lobsters and shrimp) for use as food, bait, or animal feed. They often fish hundreds of miles from shore in large boats that can hold tens of thousands of pounds of fish. Time away from their home port can last for several weeks or even months. Work on the ship is a cycle of strenuous activity followed by quiet lulls. Netting and hauling the fish in are exhausting activities that require great physical strength and endurance, but a period of rest is enjoyed when the ship sails to its home port or another fishing ground.

Most commercial fishing vessels are staffed by a crew that includes a captain, a first mate, a boatswain, and deckhands. A captain plans and supervises the entire fishing expedition. He or she draws up a budget and decides what fish will be pursued, where the crew will fish, how the fish will be caught, how long the trip will last, and how the catch will be sold upon return to port. The captain will also make sure the boat is in proper working order, buy the necessary supplies and equipment, monitor all weather information, and chart the ship's course using compasses, charts, and tables. A captain must have a thorough knowledge of navigation, boat handling skills, weather patterns, radio-telephone techniques, and the use of electronic gear. He or she must also be able to make good decisions quickly and calmly in emergencies, train and manage a crew with skill and tact, and ensure that fish are handled properly so that they can be safely eaten by consumers. Almost all captains are self-employed, and many own at least some share of their ship.

The first mate serves as the captain's assistant and operates the ship and directs the crew when the captain is off duty. The first mate also organizes and directs the actual fishing activity and sailing operations, such as gathering, preserving, storing, and unloading the catch and maintaining and repairing the ship. He or she must be able to perform all of the captain's duties as well as those of the deckhands should an emergency make his or her assistance necessary.

A boatswain acts as a supervisor of the deckhands, directing them in the performance of the ship's sailing and fishing operations. The boatswain also repairs fishing gear, equipment, and nets, if necessary. The deckhands are responsible for loading and unloading supplies and

A fisherman hauls a load of shrimp out of the waters of Ipswich Bay, Massachusetts.

equipment; untying the lines that moor a ship to the dock; letting out and hauling in the nets; cleaning, preserving, and storing the catch; unloading the catch upon return; and keeping the decks clear and clean and the ship's engines and equipment running smoothly. Deckhands must be in good health, extremely coordinated and mechanically inclined, and very strong. Most commercial fishers begin their careers as deckhands.

Fishermen use large nets spread between the main ship and a smaller boat to catch fish.

Education/Training

The most common way to get a job on a fishing boat is to "walk the docks" at the fishing ports, going from boat to boat asking captains for a job. No formal academic requirements exist, though some high schools offer two-year vocational-technical programs in commercial fishing. Many fishers learn the trade from family members already working in the industry. Operators of large commercial fishing boats must complete a Coast Guard–approved training course. In addition, some community colleges and

Did You Know...?

- Commercial fishing has one of the highest proportions of self-employed workers in the North American workforce.
- Almost all captains eventually become self-employed, and most of them will own (fully or in part) one or more fishing ships.
- A commercial fishing trip may require being at sea for several weeks or even months, often hundreds of miles from home port.
- Fishing boats are much more comfortable today than they used to be. Many modern-day boats include televisions and shower stalls.
- Roughly one out of ten commercial fishers is female.

universities offer courses in seamanship, boat operations, marine safety, navigation, boat repair and maintenance, and first aid.

Following are some training programs and vocational schools where you can begin to learn the ropes of commercial fishing:

Alaska Vocational Technical Center offers an extensive selection of classes in marine and fisheries skills. Contact AVTEC Admissions Office, P.O. Box 889, Seward, AK 99664, or call them at (907) 224-3322.

Educational Training Co., in Sitka, Alaska, offers five-day advanced survival training courses as well as land and sea survival courses for individuals, companies, communities, and schools. Contact Dug or Susan Jensen at (907) 747-3008, or e-mail survival@ptialaska.net.

Outlook

There are about 51,000 fishers and fishing boat operators nationwide. Roughly 60 percent of these individuals are self-employed. The industry is getting smaller, mainly because pollution and excessive fishing in the past have depleted fish stocks. The number of permits issued to fishers has declined in an attempt to allow fish populations to rebound. The median annual income for a fisher is $20,072, with the highest-paid 10 percent of fishers earning $40,820 and the lowest-paid 10 percent earning $10,088. Earnings tend to be highest in the summer and fall and lowest during the winter. About 75 percent of fishers work full-time for only part of the year, taking other jobs during the off-season in order to earn more money. Many of them work in fish processing plants, stores that sell fishing and boating equipment, or construction.

FOR MORE INFORMATION

ASSOCIATIONS

Atlantic Salmon Federation
Web site: http://www.asf.ca

Canadian Department of Fisheries and Oceans (DFO)
Web site: http://www.dfo-mpo.gc.ca/index.htm

Caribbean Fisheries Management Council—NOAA
Web site: http://www.caribbeanfmc.com

Marine Stewardship Council
Web site: http://www.msc.org

Ministry of Fisheries and Cooperatives
Web site: http://ncb.intnet.mu/fishco/index.htm

New England Fishery Management Council
Web site: http://www.nefmc.org

South Atlantic Fishery Management Council
Web site: http://www.safmc.nmfs.gov

U.S. Aquaculture Suppliers Association
Web site: http://www.aquaculturesuppliers.com

JOB BANKS

Alaska Fishing Jobs Clearinghouse
Web site: http://www.fishingjobs.com

Alaska Job Bank (listings by region and job specialty)
Web site: http://www.labor.state.ak.us/esjobs/jobs

Fishjobs: The Seafood Industry Jobs Network
Web site: http://www.fishjobs.com

Maritime Jobs: Maritime Employment Referral Company
Web site: http://www.maritimejobs.net

WEB SITES

Commercial Fishing News
http://www.onlinemariner.com

Commercial Fishing Today
http://interactive.usask.ca/skinteractive/modules/fisheries/
commercial/present.html

Fishing Works: All Things Fishing
http://www.FishingWorks.com

The Fish Sniffer Online
http://www.imhooked.com

National Fisherman Online
http://www.nationalfisherman.com

Sea Fishing
http://www.sea-fishing.com

BOOKS

Alaska Geographic Society, *Commercial Fishing in Alaska*, *Alaska Geographic,* vol. 24, no. 3. Anchorage, AK: Alaska Geographic Society, 1997.

Allison, Charlene J., Sue-Ellen Jacobs, and Mary A. Porter. *Winds of Change: Women in Northwest Commercial Fishing*. Seattle, WA: University of Washington Press, 1990.

Fields, Leslie Leyland. *The Entangling Net: Alaska's Commercial Fishing Women Tell Their Lives*. Urbana, IL: University of Illinois Press, 1999.

Gilmore, Janet Crofton. *The World of the Oregon Fishboat: A Study in Maritime Folklife*. Pullman, WA: Washington State University Press, 1999.

Greenlaw, Linda. *The Hungry Ocean: A Swordboat Captain's Journey*. New York: Little, Brown and Co., 1999.

Matsen, Brad. *Fishing Up North: Stories of Luck and Loss in Alaskan Waters.* Anchorage, AK: Alaska Northwest Books, 1998.

McCloskey, William. *Their Fathers' Work: Casting Nets with the World's Fishermen.* New York: McGraw-Hill Professional Publishing, 2000.

Miles, Tony, Martin Ford, Peter Gathercole, and Tony Ford. *Practical Fishing Encyclopedia.* New York: Lorenz Books, 2000.

Sainsbury, John C. *Commercial Fishing Methods: An Introduction to Vessels and Gears.* Boston, MA: Blackwell Science, Inc., 1996.

Upton, Joe. *Alaska Blues: A Season of Fishing the Inside Passage.* Seattle, WA: Sasquatch Books, 1998.

Winters, Adam. *Choosing a Career in the Fishing Industry.* New York: The Rosen Publishing Group, Inc., 2000.

Younker, Richard. *Yankin' and Liftin' Their Whole Lives: A Mississippi River Commercial Fisherman.* Carbondale, IL: Southern Illinois University Press, 2000.

MAGAZINES

Alaska Fisherman's Journal
Web site: http://www.afjournal.com

Aquaculture Magazine
Web site: http://www.aquaculturemag.com

Boats and Harbors
Web site: http://www.boats-and-harbors.com

Commercial Fisheries News
Web site: http://www.fish-news.com/cfn_home.html

The Fishermen's News
Web site: http://www.fishermensnews.com

Fish Farming News
Web site: http://www.fish-news.com/ffn.htm

Marine Yellow Pages
Web site: http://www.mypid.com

Pacific Fishing
Web site: http://www.pfmag.com
The West Coast's leading commercial fishing magazine.

World Fishing
Web site: http://www.thru.to/worldfishing

VIDEOS

Alaska the Great State of Commercial Fishing
Web site: http://www.ydot.com

MULTIMEDIA

Streaming Fish Videos
Web site: http://www.FishingWorks.com/FishingWorks.cfm?
page=CL_detail.cfm&category_id=921&part_id=5
Streaming videos on the art of fishing.

3

RANCH HAND

If you love farms, horses, and working outdoors, and have an easy-going, sociable personality, you might be cut out to be a professional ranch hand. You may fear that this is more a Hollywood fantasy than a real job, but there are lots of opportunities to work as a wrangler at either a working, family-owned cattle ranch or a dude ranch (a ranch that is open to vacationers). If you are hoping to spend your workday in some of the most majestic places in the world, look no further.

Description

The basic duties of a ranch hand—or wrangler—on a working ranch are tending livestock and repairing and cleaning fences, ranch buildings, and equipment. Tending livestock usually includes feeding, birthing, branding, shearing, roping, sorting, pasturing, herding, grooming, and doctoring the ranch's horses, cattle, poultry, pigs, and/or sheep. Having raised healthy animals through this attentive care, ranch hands must also haul the livestock to market or to a shipping terminal.

Horses are particularly crucial to the operation of a successful ranch, regardless of whether it is a working or a dude ranch. It falls to the wranglers to care for the horses on the ranch. At a working ranch, horses are used to herd cattle. At a dude ranch, the horses are usually younger and are used for taking guests riding. Because of this, their health and well-being are very important. Horse-related duties include daily brushing and grooming, tack and equipment upkeep and repair, basic veterinarian skills, fence building and repair, trail maintenance, and the maintenance and cleaning of corrals.

A wrangler herding horses

Wrangler jobs on dude ranches require not only considerable skill in horsemanship and stable operation but also good people skills, as you must be able to interact with adult guests and their children. Many ranches have access to private water sources, offering fishing opportunities as well. A good ranch guide may also be expected to take guests on overnight hiking and fishing trips or cattle drives, teach basic riding skills, lead horseback riding and river rafting expeditions, and perhaps get behind the wheel for some off-road, four-wheel drive adventures. Jobs on dude ranches

Guests practice lassoing at the Teton Valley Ranch Camp in Jackson Hole, Wyoming.

generally involve lots of hard work, long hours (usually dawn to dusk), and participation in evening activities for guests, such as line dances, cookouts, hayrides, and staff talent shows. Most northern dude ranches hire their hands during the period between November and April. Southern dude ranches hire in the August to October season. While pay is usually low, compensation often includes room and board, a share of tips, and use of the facilities and horses when off duty.

The History of Dude Ranching

Dude ranching first emerged in the late 1800s when European visitors and American tourists from the East first began to travel out West. These ranches provided safe, comfortable accommodations in beautiful and rugged settings, and gave guests a taste of what ranch life was really like. For a fee of ten dollars, guests received a full week of accommodations, hearty meals, horses to ride, and the company of ranchers. Modern-day dude ranches offer the very same pleasures (though usually at a higher rate).

Education/Training

You don't need a formal education to succeed in this line of work; hands-on experience is the best schooling. Fortunately, seasonal work is pretty easy to come by. If you hope someday to advance to ranch foreman or even own your own ranch, you should consider a community college or university degree in agricultural production, agricultural economics, animal husbandry, or veterinary medicine. Other ranch jobs to consider as a starting point include children's counselor, trails foreman, groomer, cook, wait-staff member, maintenance worker, or, in the winter months, cross-country ski instructor. Trails foremen are usually required to have a background in trail planning and building. Aside from previous work experience, the only official training you should look into getting for most of these jobs is CPR and first-aid certification.

Outlook

With dude ranches becoming an increasingly popular destination for families seeking a unique vacation, there are growing opportunities in this field. In addition, many western states, such as Texas and Wyoming, have reported shortages of ranch hands in recent years.

You have many geographic options if you wish to pursue employment as a ranch hand. Try Arizona, California, Colorado, Montana, Nevada, New Mexico, New York, Texas, Washington, Wyoming, or Hawaii. In Canada, you can try Alberta and British Columbia. And don't forget Mexico, Argentina, Brazil, and other ranch-friendly areas.

FOR MORE INFORMATION

ASSOCIATIONS

Alberta Country Vacation Association
Box 396
Sangudo, AB T0E 2A0
(403) 785-3700

Arizona Dude Ranch Association
P.O. Box 603K
Cortaro, AZ 85625

British Columbia Guest Ranch Association
P.O. Box 3301
Kamloops, BC V2C 6B9
(250) 374-6836

Colorado Dude and Guest Ranch Association
P.O. Box 2120
Granby, CO 80446
(970) 887-3128

The Dude Ranchers' Association
P.O. Box 741K
LaPorte, CO 80535
(970) 223-8440

Idaho Guest and Dude Ranch Association
HC 72 K
Cascade, ID 83611
(208) 382-4336

Montana Big Sky Ranch Association
1627 West Main Street, Suite 434K
Bozeman, MT 59715

Texas Guest Ranch Association
900 Congress Avenue, Suite 201
Austin, TX 78701
(512) 474-2996

WEB SITES

Dude Ranch and Guest Ranch Headquarters
http://www.ranchweb.com

Gene Kilgore's Online Guide to Ranch Vacations
http://www.ranchweb.com/multimedia.htm
Download a video about one of these ranches:

Hidden Creek Ranch, Harrison, ID
Quarter Circle Five Ranch, Lund, NV
Vee Bar Guest Ranch, Laramie, WY
63 Ranch, Livingston, MT
Coulter Lake Guest Ranch, Rifle, CO
Alisal Guest Ranch, Solvang, CA
Rocking C Ranch, Huntsville, UT

Summer Jobs at Dude Ranches and Guest Ranches
http://www.coolworks.com/ranch_jobs.htm

VIDEOS

Dude Ranch Days **(1999)**
PBS Home Video
Lindsay Wagner hosts this PBS video about the famous dude ranches of the West and how they preserve American history and culture.

Dude Ranches Out West: Then and Now **(1997)**
Tapeworm.
History on dude ranches of the West.

BOOKS

Dillman, Bruce. *The Cowboy Handbook*. Lincoln, NE: Lone Prairie Publishing, 1998.

Evans, Clay Bonnyman. *I Can See By Your Outfit: Becoming a Cowboy a Century Too Late*. Boulder, CO: Johnson Books, 1999.

Funke-Riehle, Felicitas, and Kendall Nelson. *Gathering Remnants: A Tribute to the Working Cowboy.* Sun Valley, ID: Prairie Creek Productions, 2001.

Howe, Robert. *Yours, from Wyoming: Letters and Stories About People and Other Wildlife from the Cowboy State*. Encampment, WY: Morningsong Publishing International, 2000.

Kilgore, Gene. *Gene Kilgore's Ranch Vacations: The Complete Guide to Guest and Resort, Fly-Fishing, and Cross-Country Skiing Ranches in the United States and Canada*. Emeryville, CA: Avalon Travel Publishing, 1999.

LeRoy, Tammy, and Robert Dawson. *Along the Cowboy Trail.* Phoenix, AZ: RD Publishing, Inc., 2000.

Markus, Kurt. *Cowpuncher*. Kalispell, MT: Wild Horse Island Press, 2000.

McCumber, David. *The Cowboy Way: Seasons on a Montana Ranch*. Austin, TX: Bard Books, 2000.

Moody, Ralph. *The Home Ranch*. Lincoln, NE: University of Nebraska Press, 1994.

Morris, Michele. *The Cowboy Life: A Saddlebag Guide for Dudes, Tenderfeet, and Cow Punchers Everywhere*. Forest City, NC: Fireside Books, 1993.

Starrs, Paul F. *Let the Cowboy Ride: Cattle Ranching in the American West*. Baltimore, MD: Johns Hopkins Press, 2000.

Stoecklein, David R. *Don't Fence Me In: Images of the Spirit of the West*. Sun Valley, ID: Stoecklein Publications, 1996.

ECOTOURISM PLANNER

Ecotourism is fairly new. The term refers to trips to exotic or remote locales that are not often frequented by tourists, such as the Arctic Circle or Brazilian rain forests. The real key to ecotours, though, is that while the adventure should enrich the traveler, it must not damage the ecosystem of the place being visited, and it should be economically beneficial to the local people.

This is the right time to be getting into ecotourism. Every year the industry grows significantly, and 2002 has been declared the International Year of Ecotourism by the United Nations. As ecotours continue to grow in popularity with adventurous and thoughtful travelers worldwide, the employment opportunities within the industry for people who want to lead or organize tours in wild and uncharted places become ever greater.

Description

To be successful in this field, you will need good communication skills, the ability to work independently and creatively, and a sense of adventure. Although you do not need to go to school to prepare, you should be willing to do lots of your own research, both through reading and by visiting the places where you someday wish to lead tours. Once you are well informed and are knowledgeable in your chosen area of expertise, you can begin guiding ecotours for an established and reputable ecotour operator or even start your own company.

Tourism is now the world's largest industry. As much as 60 percent of this industry is devoted to tourists whose main travel goal is to enjoy and appreciate nature. For an increasing number of countries, tourism based on natural attractions is the leading source of national revenue. As a result, ecotourism is promoted more every year, and its

Students listen to a guide explain buttress roots in a rain forest at Yacumama Lodge in Iquitos, Peru.

economic importance has grown in equal measure. Because people are now realizing that there is money to be made in this field, ecotourism has given governments and local residents powerful incentives to conserve natural and cultural resources. Often, a happy by-product of ecotourism is the development and enrichment of communities that have traditionally been impoverished. For all these reasons, many individuals, organizations, and governments are getting behind ecotourism. As a result, there are many new opportunities for an adventurous person to launch a career in ecotourism, allowing her or him a chance to make a good living, see the world, and work toward a good cause—ecological conservation and community development.

As an ecotravel guide or tour operator, there are several principles and practices you would be expected to adopt. You must develop an understanding of and respect for the complex interactions of plants, animals, and humans. As a guide, you must be knowledgeable and entertaining, and be able to transform hard science and ancient history into accessible, interesting talks. You should try to involve local people as much as possible in your tours and encourage your travelers to support local businesses. As well, you should fill as many job positions as possible with local employees who ordinarily have very limited economic opportunities. In this way, local residents will clearly see the value of preserving their environment and the travelers you lead will learn about the customs, traditions, and languages of their hosts. Above all, you should avoid or minimize any environmental harm to fragile ecosystems and encourage your travelers to join organizations that support preservation and protect the rights of indigenous peoples around the world.

Street vendors tend to their fare at a local market in Antigua, Guatemala.

Education/Training

Robert Smith, owner of the ecotour company Timbuktours, advises getting a background in first aid, natural interpretation, and other basic skills before embarking on a career in ecotourism. He believes that getting a degree is not necessary and that a few background courses are more than enough.

"Many secondary education institutions and universities offer short-term courses and certification programs that apply directly to the eco- and adventure tourism industry," he says.

The International Ecotourism Society (TIES) offers training in this field in the form of forums, field seminars, and workshops. Park rangers, landscape architects, and other nature professionals from dozens of countries around the globe attend its events.

Profile

Robert Smith, ecotour guide
Owner, Timbuktours

WHY IS ECOTOURISM SO POPULAR?

With so many frontiers in a rapidly developing market, the time to take advantage of these opportunities would be now, while regulation is more or less wide open. Because many people are increasingly feeling a need to interact with the natural environment, ecotourism will become more and more popular.

HOW DID YOU GET INVOLVED IN THIS UNIQUE INDUSTRY?

I've been a guide ever since I can remember, venturing alone or with friends into the bush in my native South Africa. Alone, I was guided by my instincts, intuition, and knowledge, and I was usually the appointed leader when venturing outdoors. My know-how, or bushwhacking ability, was first gained by being a Boy Scout as a youth, and later as an infantryman in the military. I also learned a lot from an uncle who was a nature conservationist.

WHY DID YOU START YOUR OWN COMPANY?

Because of the understanding I have of the natural world, I am definitely in favor of "treading lightly" and the "leave no trace" protocol. This explains my affiliation with eco-tourism, which allows people to get closer to the environment with much less intrusion than conventional forms of tourism.

Today I operate as an eco/adventure guide and wilderness interpreter in the Republic of South Africa, Canada, and in other countries. With hiking, camping, ocean kayaking, and river rafting as my means for giving my clients the kind of travel experience they will never forget, I have created the opportunity for myself to work and play hard simultaneously.

WHAT ADVICE COULD YOU GIVE YOUNG PEOPLE WHO SHARE YOUR INTERESTS?

If you are the same kind of person as I am, then ecotourism is your ticket to a rewarding career. Many people finish high school and do not have a very clear realization of what they intend to do with their lives afterwards. After all, this is a rather big decision to make. There are not many alternatives to the rat race. However, with the rapid and large-scale expansion of tourism, there are some opportunities to be found.

FOR MORE INFORMATION

ASSOCIATIONS

Conservation International
1919 M Street NW
Suite 600
Washington, DC 20036
(202) 912-1000
(800) 406-2306
e-mail: d.vizcaino@conservation.org
Web site: http://www.conservation.org
http://www.ecotour.org

Eco Tourism International
11611 East Berry Avenue
Englewood, CO 80111
(720) 554-0333
e-mail: ed_sanders@attglobal.net
Web site: http://www.kcv.com/eti

Ecoventura/Galapagos Network
6303 Blue Lagoon Drive, Suite 140
Miami, FL 33126
(305) 262-6264
(800) 633-7972
e-mail: info@galapagosnetwork.com
Web site: http://www.ecoventura.com

Galapagos Explorer II/Kapawi Lodge
2735 P.O. Box 59-9000
Miami, FL 33159-9000
(593) 428-5711
e-mail: abarona@canodros.com
Web site: http://www.canodros.com

International Ecotourism Club
P.O. Box 65232
Psihico, 15410
Athens, Greece
+30 1 671 9671
e-mail: a@ecoclub.com
Web site: http://www.ecoclub.com

Manaca, Inc.
1609 Connecticut Avenue NW
4th Floor
Washington, DC 20009
(202) 265-8204
e-mail: andreas@manaca.com
Web site: http://www.manaca.com

Naturalist.com Network/Wilderness Web
24 White Place
Burlington, VT 05401
(888) 277-7622
e-mail: explore@wildernessweb.com
Web site: http://www.naturalist.com
http://www.wildernessweb.com

Programme for Belize
1 Eyre Street
Belize City, Belize
(501) 275 616
e-mail: pfbel@btl.net
Web site: http://www.pfbelize.org

Temptress Adventure Cruises
6100 Hollywood Boulevard, Suite 202
Hollywood, FL 33024
(954) 983-2989
(800) 336-8423
e-mail: info@temptresscruises.com
Web site: http://www.temptresscruises.com

Turismo da Natureza Portugal
Av. Eng. Arantes e Oliveira n.
13, 4 B
Lisboa, 1900-221 Portugal
+351 21 841 8743
e-mail: rui.marques@icat.fc.ul.pt
Web site: http://www.icat.fc.ul.pt

World Explorer Cruises
555 Montgomery Street, #1400
San Francisco, CA 94111-2544
(415) 820-9200
e-mail: wec@wecruise.com
Web site: http://www.wecruise.com

PROGRAMS

The International Ecotourism Society (TIES) Training Opportunities
TIES offers specialized programs in coordination with:
• University-based programs: For training partnerships with universities, TIES is generally responsible for curriculum development and course implementation, while the university coordinates publicity and registration for the course.
• Government and NGO-sponsored programs: TIES designs curricula that can be used as part of ecotourism training programs for host governments and non-government organizations (NGOs) interested in upgrading the skills of local professionals in the field of ecotourism.

• Private-sector sponsored programs: TIES provides tailored training programs to the personnel of specific tourism companies.

WEB SITES

Ecotourism electronic newsletter
http://ecotourism.cc/r/news.html

Guide to EcoTravel
http://www.naturalist.com/channels/Ecotravel

International Ecotourism Society
http://www.ecotourism.org

Lindblad Expeditions
http://www.expeditions.com

Nature Travel EcoVolunteer
http://www.ecovolunteer.org

BOOKS

Honey, Martha. *Ecotourism and Sustainable Development: Who Owns Paradise?* Washington, DC: Island Press, 1999.

Lindberg, Kreg, ed. *Ecotourism: A Guide for Planners and Managers*. North Bennington, VT: Ecotourism Society, 1993.

Lindberg, Kreg, ed. *Ecotourism: A Guide for Planners and Managers, Vol. II*. North Bennington, VT: Ecotourism Society, 1998.

McLaren, Deborah. *Rethinking Tourism and Ecotravel: The Paving of Paradise and What You Can Do to Stop It*. West Hartford, CT: Kumarian Press, 1997.

Middleton, Victor T. C., and Rebecca Hawkins. *Sustainable Tourism: A Marketing Perspective*. Woburn, MA: Butterworth-Heinemann, 2000.

Mowforth, Martin. *Tourism and Sustainability: New Tourism in the Third World*. New York: Routledge, 1998.

Neale, Greg, ed. *The Green Travel Guide*. Sterling, VA: Stylus Publishing, 1999.

Patterson, Carol. *The Business of Ecotourism*. Rhinelander, WI: Explorers Guide Publishing, 1997.

Wearing, Stephen, and John Neil. *Ecotourism: Impacts, Potentials, and Possibilities*. Woburn, MA: Butterworth-Heinemann, 1999.

The design and maintenance of lawns and gardens sometimes involve topiary art—cutting and trimming trees into original or ornamental shapes.

Most entry-level jobs in the industry require no college education; in fact, almost half of new hires do not yet have a high school diploma. Instead, training in landscaping techniques and the use of mowers, trimmers, leaf blowers, and tractors occurs on the job. Wages tend to be low (entry-level landscaping and groundskeeping laborers receive an average of $8.24 an hour, while managers make about $12 an hour), but for nature lovers the paycheck is offset by the days spent outside, the varied workday, and the satisfaction of participating in the beautification of one's surroundings.

Nursery and greenhouse workers grow the plants, flowers, shrubs, and trees that will eventually be planted by landscapers. Landscape contractors turn the designs of landscape architects into reality. They supervise the planting of trees, shrubs, and flowers; the laying of sod; and the placement of benches, statuary, and other design elements. They may also install lighting and sprinkler systems and build footpaths, patios, decks, and fountains. They may work only on large commercial projects, such as office complexes, corporate parks, and malls, or they may offer their services to private residences. The landscape contractor directs a supervisor who in turn oversees the landscape laborers who actually perform all the grounds work.

Groundskeeping laborers tend to focus on the maintenance of facilities, such as playing fields, golf courses, parks, college campuses, and cemeteries. Their duties are often identical to those of landscape laborers but may also include clearing snow from walkways and parking lots; maintaining and repairing sidewalks, planters, fountains, pools, fences, and benches; turf care and painting; and, in the case of cemetery laborers, digging graves with a backhoe and preparing and maintaining burial plots.

Seeing the result of his or her work is perhaps one of the most rewarding benefits of a groundskeeper's job.

Outlook

Every landowning entity (including corporations, amusement parks, professional sports organizations, the government, public institutions like schools and universities, home owners, apartment complexes, and city parks) has a need for beautification and the upkeep of its grounds. Demand is increasing for landscaping and groundskeeping services as construction of commercial and industrial complexes, homes, parks, and highways has continued to

Hello, sports fans!

One major segment of the groundskeeping industry is tending to the very particular needs of athletic fields, especially those used by professional athletes. This includes the grounds that football, baseball, golf, and tennis are played on. The grass or turf must be perfectly maintained and properly drained through the use of tractors, aerators, fertilizers, and insecticides. Astroturf must be vacuumed and disinfected. Groundskeepers who care for athletic fields keep natural and artificial turf fields in top condition, mark out boundaries, and paint turf with team logos and names before events take place. Workers who maintain golf courses are called greenskeepers. They do many of the same things other groundskeepers do, but they may also relocate the holes on putting greens and repair and paint ball washers, benches, and tee markers. Imagine the satisfaction of seeing your handiwork on television while your favorite team plays on the field you have tended with such care!

grow. In addition, turnover among landscapers and groundskeepers is high, so it is usually easy to find an entry-level job. This means groundskeepers can find satisfying work in just about any location: urban, rural, or suburban. You can work as part of the groundskeeping staff at a large institution, for a private contractor, or even go into business for yourself.

Education/Training

Typically, groundskeepers must have a high school diploma (or the equivalent) and a driver's license, and should be able to demonstrate literacy and good interpersonal skills. The best education is the one you get by observing more experienced workers on the job and by getting your hands dirty. You will learn skills like planting, cultivating, and pruning trees, and fertilizing lawns, trees, and shrubs, as well as how to operate equipment. Inexpensive courses in gardening and horticulture are often available at nurseries and greenhouses, and will provide a solid background for your career.

Many high school and two-year vocational/technical school graduates as well as retirees are entering this field, according to the PLCAA. The American Society of Landscape Architects' (ASLA) National Certification Program offers exams and certification for landscape professionals.

FOR MORE INFORMATION

ASSOCIATIONS

American Institute of Certified Planners
1776 Massachusetts Avenue NW, #400
Washington, DC 20036
(202) 872-0611
Web site: http://www.planning.org

American Landscape Maintenance Association
737 Hollywood Boulevard
Hollywood, FL 33019
(954) 927-3100

American Nursery and Landscape Association
1250 I Street NW, Suite 500
Washington, DC 20005-3922
(202) 789-2900
Web site: http://www.anla.org

American Society of Agronomy
677 South Segoe Road
Madison, WI 53711
(608) 273-8080
e-mail: headquarters@Agronomy.org
Web site: http://www.Agronomy.org

American Society of Landscape Architects
908 North Second Street
Harrisburg, PA 17102
(717) 236-2044
Web site: http://www.landscapearchitects.org

Associated Landscape Contractors of America, Inc.
150 Elden Street, Suite 270
Herndon, VA 20170
Web site: http://www.alca.org

California Landscape & Irrigation Council Inc.
4195 Chino Hills Parkway
Suite 398
Chino Hills, CA 91709
(909) 393-2114
e-mail: clic@att.net

Canadian Nursery Landscape Association
Institute of Groundsmanship
Web site: http://www.iog.org

Landscape Contractors Association of MD-DC-VA
15245 Shady Grove Road, Suite 130
Rockville, MD 20850
(301) 948-0810
e-mail: lca@mgmtsol.com

National Institute on Park & Grounds Management
730 W. Frances Street
Appleton, WI 54914-2365
e-mail: nipgm@tpo.org

National Recreation & Park Association
22377 Belmont Ridge Road
Ashburn, VA 20148
(540) 858-0784
(800) 626-6772
e-mail: info@nrpa.org

Professional Grounds Management Society
720 Light Street
Baltimore, MD 21230

(800) 609-7467
Web site: http://www.pgms.org

Sports Turf Managers Association
1375 Rolling Hills Loop
Council Bluffs, IA 51503-8552
(800) 323-3875
Web site: http://www.sportsturfmanager.com

Turf and Ornamental Communicators Association (TOCA)
120 W. Main Street
P.O. Box 156
New Prague, MN 56071
(612) 758-6340
Web site: http://www.toca.org

WEB SITES

Groundskeeper University
http://www.groundskeeper.com

LandscapeOnline
http://www.landscapeonline.com

Plant Healthcare **online magazine**
http://www.planthealthcare.com

State of the Industry Report 2000 (from *Lawn and Landscape Magazine*)
http://www.lawnandlandscape.com/articles

MAGAZINES

Landscape Management: Solutions for a Growing Industry
Web site: http://www.landscapemanagement.net

Lawn and Landscape Magazine
Web site: http://www.lawnandlandscape.com

BOOKS

Armitage, Allan M. *Armitage's Garden Perennials: A Color Encyclopedia*. Portland, OR: Timber Press, 2000.

Buchanan, Rita. *Taylor's Master Guide to Landscaping*. Boston, MA: Houghton Mifflin, 2000.

Dirr, Michael A. *Dirr's Hardy Trees and Shrubs: An Illustrated Encyclopedia*. Portland, OR: Timber Press, 1997.

Dirr, Michael A. *Manual of Woody Landscape Plants.* Champaign, IL: Stipes Publishing, 1998.

Gilman, Dr. Edward E. *An Illustrated Guide to Pruning*. Florence, KY: Delmar Publishers, 1997.

Gilman, Dr. Edward E. *Trees for Urban and Suburban Landscapes*. Florence, KY: Delmar Publishers, 1997.

Still, Steven. *Manual of Herbaceous Ornamental Plants*. Champaign, IL: Stipes Publishing, 1993.

Taylor, Norman. *Taylor's Guide to Annuals*. Boston, MA: Houghton Mifflin, 2000.

Taylor, Norman. *Taylor's Guide to Ornamental Grasses*. Boston, MA: Houghton Mifflin, 1997.

von Trapp, Sara Jane. *Landscaping from the Ground* Up. Newtown, CT: Taunton Press, 1997.

Ware, George W. *Complete Guide to Pest Control With and Without Chemicals.* Fresno, CA: Thomson Publications, 1996.

TEACHER/ NATURALIST

Though close observation of nature is as old as humanity itself, the methodical, codified system of its study that we use today is less than 300 years old. The formal study of nature that was created and adopted by scientists and amateur science enthusiasts, who became known as naturalists, began in England with the Reverend Gilbert White, who was born in 1720. Today the term "naturalist" has several meanings. Teacher/naturalists are community outreach leaders, educators, nature experts, writers, and explorers, all rolled into one. Although some positions require naturalists to hold an advanced degree, there are many opportunities for self-education and advancement through hands-on experience in this fascinating and rewarding career.

Description

Often, the title of this job is "teacher/naturalist" or "instructor/naturalist." This type of job is most commonly found at nature centers or preservation associations. You may also find employment at zoos, zoological gardens, or summer camps. Naturalists provide natural science programs to schools, interested groups, and the general public. Most teacher/naturalists fulfill many functions during the course of a single workday; their job requires them to serve as writers (of articles, brochures, and explanatory text on walls or posted near trails), teachers, historians, and mentors. They often lead field trips for visiting schoolchildren and deliver presentations in schools. Naturalists plan, organize, and conduct bird-watching expeditions, nature walks, seminars on outdoor skills, and nature-inspired craft classes. They can even get involved in land-use decisions concerning the parks in which they work; their opinion may be sought on

Hikers walk up a steep path in the Sacred Valley of the Incas in Peru.

what trees should be cut, how and where trails should be constructed, and where and if additional campsites should be built.

Because there is very little money to be made as a teacher/naturalist, you must have a genuine love for nature, its study, and its enjoyment. You should have a real curiosity about the natural world and how it works and a real desire to share what you learn with others. Needless to say, you should be physically fit and active. Having a sense of creativity and initiative is also useful; this will make the programs you create, the articles and interpretive texts you write, and the talks you deliver far more interesting and informative to a wide audience. You will also have to be flexible. You will often have to work on weekends and at night (when most of the public finally has time for camping, hiking, biking, and stargazing). Naturalist jobs are not very plentiful, so you should be prepared to relocate if necessary.

Education/Training

As positions vary in this field, so do qualification requirements. For example, naturalists at the New Jersey Audubon Society (NJAS) are required to have some knowledge of natural history, a background in education, excellent communications and time-management skills, and a cooperative attitude. NJAS believes that for a naturalist position, field experience is more valuable than a degree in natural science, and the necessary formal education can be attained through many of its own projects and not-for-credit workshops. Internships are another great way to gain hands-on experience in this field. Many nature centers and zoos employ interns to provide opportunities for individuals to gain experience in the field of natural science. Working as an intern or volunteering at a park, nature center, zoo, museum, or camp can be useful training and may eventually lead to a paying job. Some high schools, such as

A naturalist sets up a naked mole rat exhibit at the Burnet Park Zoo in Syracuse, New York.

North Hollywood High School in Los Angeles, California, and the High School for Environmental Studies in New York City, offer a program of classes on ecology. These classes cover agriculture, environmental science, Latin, personal and planetary health, ecology, systems theory, economics, and botany. It is a very good idea to take some environmental studies courses that are offered at your local community college. The more formal education you have, the more employable you will be.

Farber, Paul Lawrence. *Finding Order in Nature: The Naturalist Tradition from Linnaeus to E. O. Wilson*. Baltimore, MD: Johns Hopkins University Press, 2000.

Maynard, Thane. *Working with Wildlife: A Guide to Careers in the Animal World*. New York: Franklin Watts, 2000.

Miller, Louise. *Careers for Animal Lovers*. Lincolnwood, IL: VGM Career Horizons, 1991.

Pielou, E. C. *A Naturalist's Guide to the Arctic*. Chicago: University of Chicago Press, 1994.

Sibley, Edith A. *Nature with Children of All Ages: Activities for Exploring, Learning, and Enjoying the World Around Us*. Englewood, NJ: Prentice Hall, Inc., 1982.

JOURNALS AND MAGAZINES

American Midland Naturalist
P.O. Box 369
Notre Dame, IN 46556-0369
(219) 631-7481
e-mail: ammidnat.1@nd.edu

The American Naturalist
Web site: http://www.journals.uchicago.edu/AN/home.html

Refuge Reporter
Avocet Crossing
Millwood, VA 22646-0156
(540) 837-2152
e-mail:refrep@mnsinc.com
Web site: http://www.gorp.com/refrep
An independent journal to increase recognition and support for the National Wildlife Refuge System.

Western Birder and Naturalist Magazine
Web site: http://www.westernbirder.com

WildBird Magazine
Fancy Publications, Inc.
P.O. Box 6050
Mission Viejo, CA 92690
(714) 855-8822
A magazine dedicated to bird-watching.

Wilderness Way
P.O. Box 203
Lufkin, TX 75904-0203
(409) 632-8746
This magazine covers many topics: survival skills, outdoor activities, primitive and historical ways of life, culture, earth medicine, and Native American studies.

VIDEOS

Tracking: Mastering the Basics, **by Dr. James Halfpenny (1997)**
Four-part video series covering tracking process and footprint identification, field techniques, gaits and gait patterns, and interpreting stories.

MULTIMEDIA

90 Second Naturalist (Web radio show)
Web site: http://www.nsnaturalist.org

cities. Much of your day will probably be spent outside, exposed to the elements and weather patterns associated with these types of terrain.

Education/Training

Experience supplemented with some form of training is the way to go here; no formal college education is necessary. Field experience is very valuable and will set you apart from other high school graduates. You can volunteer or intern at a nature center, outdoor education center, or state or national park to get experience in the field and find out which duties or geographic areas you prefer. Try contacting your local forester, wildlife manager, or naturalist to inquire about such opportunities.

Many park rangers break into entry-level positions after high school, beginning their careers as seasonal rangers (or as volunteers). Seasonal rangers either work in one park for part of the year or travel from park to park, working at one in the winter and another in the summer. They usually perform the ranger equivalent of grunt work, such as toll collecting, cleaning campsites, maintaining trails, staffing information desks, and guiding tours. They receive few if any benefits. You may have to work as a seasonal ranger for several years before a full-time position becomes available. Once you win this job, however, you will enjoy good job

National Park Service park rangers examine wildlife in a pond in Smithfield, Rhode Island.

security and greater stability. Most full-time park rangers remain at the same park for many years.

The orientation and training a ranger receives on the job is sometimes supplemented with formal training courses. Training for duties that are unique to the National Park Service is available at the Horace M. Albright Training Center at Grand Canyon National Park, Arizona, and at the Stephen T. Mather Training Center at Harpers Ferry, West Virginia. It is also a good idea to take courses in environmental sciences, park management, natural history,

EEK! Environmental Education for Kids
http://www.dnr.state.wi.us/org/caer/ce/eek/job/ranger.htm
Diary of a park ranger.

National Park Service
http://www.nps.gov
The National Park Service site has all the information you need on pursuing a career as a park ranger and the various duties and geographic locations available to you.

Natural Resources Defense Council
http://www.nrdc.org
The Amicus Journal online is a good source of information on wildlife preservation.

BOOKS

Burby, Liza N. *A Day in the Life of a Park Ranger.* New York: The Rosen Publishing Group, Inc., 1999.

Flanagan, Alice. *Exploring Parks with Ranger Dockett.* New York: Children's Press, 1997.

Muench, David, James R. Udall, and Stewart L. Udall. *National Parks of America.* Portland, OR: Graphic Arts Center Publishing Co., 1993.

National Geographic Society, eds. *America's Hidden Treasures: Exploring Our Little-Known National Parks.* Washington, DC: National Geographic Society, 1997.

National Geographic Society, eds. *National Geographic's Guide to National Parks of the United States.* Washington, DC: National Geographic Society, 2001.

O'Gara, Geoff. *Frommer's Yellowstone and Grand Teton National Parks.* New York: IDG Books Worldwide, 2000.

Rudman, Jack. *Urban Park Ranger.* Syossett, NY: National Learning Corporation, 1988.

Wallace, Gordon. *My Ranger Years: Sequoia National Park, 1935–47.* Three Rivers, CA: Sequois Natural History Association, 1992.

MAGAZINES

New World Journal
330 W. 56th Street, Suite 3G
New York, NY 10019-4244
(212) 265-7970
Broad-based environmental magazine.

Summit
Summit Publications, Inc.
1221 May St.
Hood River, OR 97031
(503) 387-2200
Magazine promoting mountains, culture, environment, and adventure.

Wilderness Trails
Wilderness Trails, Inc.
712 Satori Drive
Petaluma, CA 94954
(707) 762-8839
Magazine for outdoor activists—combines outdoor adventure and environmental concerns.

WHALE WATCHER

Can you imagine yourself aboard a ship, sailing the seven seas like a character out of a story, while peacefully pursuing whales in their natural habitat and guiding passengers on a nautical adventure they will never forget? Whale-watching crews provide an important service to the public, help raise money for nature conservation, and enjoy one of the most awe-inspiring careers available.

Description

Whale watching, as a commercial activity, began in 1955 in North America along the southern California coast. Today, whale-watching tours sail the oceans and bays of some seventy countries and represent one of the fastest growing of all global tourism sectors. The Whale and Dolphin Conservation Society (WDCS) specifies that a safe whale-watch boat features an experienced skipper and a crew who are well trained in first aid and rescue skills. As a member of the crew, you are responsible for educating the passengers on board about the whales and other marine life observed on your outing. Many whale-watching operations invite research scientists on board, so you may also be involved in research projects with the naturalists who form part of your group.

According to the WDCS, a good guide will demonstrate several valuable characteristics. She or he should be lively and entertaining, knowledgeable about all local marine life, and able to interpret the behavior of whales spotted on the outing, including the whales' singing and mating practices. A guide should also encourage guests to become interested in conservation and point them to further sources of information on whales, such as nearby museums, bookstores, and

The skeletons of a humpback whale and a blue whale hang from the ceiling of the Whaling Museum in New Bedford, Massachusetts.

science centers. Above all, whale-watching guides should care about both the whales and their guests. The welfare of the whales should be the top priority; a whale should never be disturbed or endangered in order to give guests a closer view or bigger thrill, nor should the lives of passengers be threatened by reckless behavior.

Education/Training

Learning by doing is the key here, but you may need to do a little digging to find an operation with enough resources

Whale watchers get a close look at a gray whale in the San Ignacio Lagoon in Baja, California.

to offer you a valuable internship. The Isle of Shoals, northern New England's oldest whale-watching company, promotes an internship program that teaches students of all ages and backgrounds about sea life and how it fits into the larger ecological picture. Interns in this program act as apprentices to more experienced guides and then lead small tour groups themselves. This type of experience is a wonderful opportunity to learn all about field identification of various species, practice research and observation methods, and gain marine navigation and communication skills. Best of all, you don't need any

Fun Facts About Whales

Most large whales travel in small schools (called pods), but some swim in pairs or even alone. Whales are most often observed in open ocean during their migration from feeding to breeding grounds, a voyage of several thousands of miles.

- Watching whales as they migrate is a fascinating experience. Each winter, California gray whales travel down the Pacific coast from their summer feeding grounds in the Bering Sea and Arctic Ocean to Mexico's Baja Peninsula, where they breed and give birth. It is the longest mammal migration on Earth—12,000 miles round trip each year!

- On your whale watches, you may observe the whales eating. A blue whale eats a lot of krill, or plankton—up to the equivalent of a fully grown African elephant every day.

FOR MORE INFORMATION

WHALE WATCHING LOCATION DIRECTORY

Whales can be spotted in their natural habitats all around the world. Can you blame the whales for choosing these beautiful, often awe-inspiring places to live?

Andenes, Norway

Antarctica

Argentina

Baja California, Mexico

Brazil

British Virgin Islands

Churchill, Manitoba

Colombia

Dominican Republic

Ecuador

Hawaii

Lambert's Bay, South Africa

Monkey Mia, Western Australia

Moray Firth, Scotland

New Zealand

Ogasawara Islands, Japan

Península Valdés, Patagonia, Argentina

St. Lawrence River and the Gulf of St. Lawrence, Quebec

San Juan Islands

Tañon Strait, the Philippines

Washington State

WEB SITES

Gorp.com
http://www.gorp.com/gorp/interact/guests/ellis.htm
A forum of whale questions answered by expert Richard Ellis.

Greenpeace Global Whale Sanctuary
http://www.greenpeace.org.au/globalwhalesanctuary/index.html

White-water rafting on the Salmon River in Idaho

his or her staff and customers with shoddy equipment and negligent practices.

The best route to landing a good guide job, then, is to sign up for a rafting course. It is a relatively small investment and an awful lot of fun. Gaining this formal experience will increase your chances of getting hired by one of the better outfitters, from whom you will learn good business and rafting practices. This in turn may allow you to start your own river tour company someday. As Ken Streater says, "It's better to start earning money in your own right than to be stuck in a corporation mentality."

The river guide school you choose should be staffed by experienced, knowledgeable teachers and mentors. They should have decades of experience leading trips and teaching students. Every aspect of guiding a raft down river should be taught, from "reading" white water (predicting its flow and strength based on its surface appearance), maneuvering boats, and knot tying, to safe food preparation, composting, and recycling. The cost of a six- to eight-day course can range from about $500 to $1,000. A workshop on swift water emergency and rescue techniques should be included in your course. In this section, you will unwrap rafts, perform flipped-raft drills, use flip lines (to right an upended raft) and throw bags (for flotation), swim in rapids, swim in and out of eddies, practice foot-entrapment exercises and linecrossing of rapids, learn about hypothermia prevention and treatment, and study the other skills needed to manage a white-water emergency. Generally, students must supply some of their own gear, such as a tent, a sleeping bag, a sleeping pad, wet and dry suits, river shoes, and outdoor clothing.

A good river school will maintain a high instructor-to-student ratio (such as one to four or five) in order to ensure individual attention. Carefully supervised solo river sessions should be coupled with more hands-on instruction; this allows students to put theory into practice and discover solutions to problems on their own, thereby giving them the

A team of rescue workers search for missing people in the Saxeten brook near Interlaken, Switzerland.

confidence they will need to lead their own expeditions later on. Some schools recommend that students take a course in first aid and CPR (check with the local American Red Cross to find classes) and read about river running before enrolling in a training program. The Whitewater Voyages Guide School also recommends that potential guides spend a day playing around in an oar boat on a lake—practicing sitting, holding the oars, and being comfortable in the boat—before taking on any rapids.

A River Guide's Safety Code

As a river guide, you will have to observe certain safety codes for white-water rafting. Here are some of the guidelines:

- Make sure you and your party are all competent swimmers.
- Be sure everyone is wearing a life preserver, shoulder protection, and a correctly fitted helmet.
- Do not enter a rapid unless you are reasonably sure that you can get through it without injury or mishap.
- Make sure that each boat contains at least three people and that a party contains no less than two boats. Never boat alone.
- Have a realistic sense of your skills and the ability of your guests (taking into account their fitness, age, anxiety levels, and health). Do not attempt to navigate rapids that are beyond your party's abilities.
- Be knowledgeable in rescue and self-rescue skills, CPR, and first aid. Carry the equipment necessary for unexpected emergencies, such as knives, whistles, flashlights, folding saws, guidebooks, maps, food, waterproof matches, extra clothing, and repair kits.

(continued)

Destination Wilderness
Web site: http://www.wildernesstrips.com
This is Ken Streater's company, which specializes in wilderness rafting, kayaking, trekking, culture, and wildlife journeys in the most incredible places on Earth.

Whitewater Voyages Guide School
Web site http://www.whitewatervoyages.com/schools/wwschools.html
Intensive workshops and instruction in guiding oar and paddle rafts, encompassing fundamental skills of reading white water and maneuvering boats.

WEB SITES

E-Raft.com
http://www.e-raft.com/default.htm
E-Raft is an excellent, comprehensive online resource for white-water rafting throughout North America.

GORP.com
http://www.gorp.com/gorp/activity/paddling/pad_guid.htm
Just name your destination: GORP.com has a map of the world that features all the best rivers you can take on.

Riversearch.com
http://www.riversearch.com
Excellent Web log of the top sites for white-water trips and companies all over the world.

Wild Water Ltd.
http://www.wildwaterrafting.com
Wild Water Rafting is your guide to white-water rafting in the southeastern United States.

BOOKS

Armstead, Lloyd Dean. *Whitewater Rafting in North America*. Guilford, CT: Globe Pequot Press, 1997.

Bechdel, Les. *River Rescue: A Manual for Whitewater Safety*. Boston: Appalachian Mountain Club Books, 1997.

Bennett, Jeff. *The Complete Whitewater Rafter*. New York: McGraw-Hill, 1996.

Evans, Jay, and Eric Evans. *The Kayaking Book*. New York: Penguin Books, 1993.

Getchell, Annie. *The Essential Outdoor Gear Manual.* New York: McGraw-Hill, 2000.

Johnson, Jimmie. *Whitewater Rafting Manual: Tactics and Techniques for Great River Adventures*. Mechanicsburg, PA: Stackpole Books, 1994.

Kuhne, Cecil. *Whitewater Rafting: An Introductory Guide*. New York: Lyons Press, 1995.

Mason, Paul, and Mark Scriver. *Thrill of the Paddle: The Art of Whitewater Canoeing*. Westport, CT: Firefly Books, 1999.

Nelson, Melinda, and Rosemary Wallner. *Imagine You Are a Whitewater Rafter*. Edina, MN: Abdo and Daughters, 2001.

Wallach, Jeff. *What the River Says: Whitewater Journeys Along the Inner Frontier*. Portland, OR: Blue Heron Publishing, 1996.

MAGAZINES

Che-Mun
The Journal of Canadian Wilderness Canoeing
Box 548, Station O
Toronto, ON M4A 2P1
(416) 789-2142
e-mail: mpeake@inforamp.net

Kayak Magazine
309 Edgeway Loop
Fayetteville, NC 28314
Web site: http://www.kayakmagazine.comj116

Fighting Fires from the Sky

Smoke jumpers are firefighters who parachute into burning forests in order to fight blazes. They are flown into the remote areas that hotshot crews and other firefighters cannot reach. They jump in groups of two to ten people, with each person carrying 100 pounds of equipment on his or her back, and they fight the fire for three to five days. When finished, they gather up their equipment and hike to the nearest access road, which is often many miles away. Smoke jumpers are drawn

Smoke jumpers stand by the edge of the firebreak and put out new fires that flare up.

from the ranks of experienced firefighters from the Forest Service, Bureau of Land Management, or state forest fire departments. They often also have experience as farmers, park rangers, or ranchers. Would-be smoke jumpers must be physically fit and successfully complete a boot camp–style training session. Smoke jumpers say the pay is good, but it is the scenery, adventure, and strong sense of camaraderie that keeps them coming back year after year.

you to the forest supervisor, you will then be considered for employment on a crew. Fire managers start at about $9 per hour with experienced veterans earning as much as $16 an hour. A top salary would be about $25,000 for a six-month stint.

Education/Training

You must be knowledgeable in basic first aid and CPR before you even inquire about one of these high-risk positions.

Entry-level positions can be difficult to snare in this field. One method is to start out as a forestry aide or technician; consider these lower-rung positions as a kind of internship. These jobs can consist of backbreaking work when a forest is filled with too much growth and brush. As a result, controlled burns are now part of national forest policy.

Land managers must balance wildland fire suppression with the beneficial use of fire for resource management. A prescribed fire is any fire intentionally ignited to reduce flammable fuels, such as the accumulation of brush and logs on forest floors, or to help restore ecosystem health.

FOR MORE INFORMATION

ASSOCIATIONS
International Association of Fire Fighters
Web site: http://www.iaff.org

WEB SITES
California Professional Firefighters
http://www.cpf.org/jacinterest.htm

Colorado Wildfire Academy
http://www.cowildfireacademy.com

Fire Careers/Training
http://www.nps.gov/fire/wildland/jobs.htm

The Firefighters Bookstore
http://www.firebooks.com

Firenet (National Park Service)
http://www.nps.gov/fire/index.htm

National Firefighting Hall of Heroes
http://www.hallofflame.org/hallhero.htm

Wildfire News
http://www.wildfirenews.com

Women Firefighters Resource Page
http://www.wfsi.org

Women in the Fire Service Inc.
http://www.wfsi.org/WFS.wildjob.html

BOOKS

Beil, Karen Magnuson. *Fire in Their Eyes: Wildfires and the People Who Fight Them*. New York: Harcourt Brace, 1999.

Fritz, Richard A. *Tools of the Trade: Firefighting Hand Tools and Their Use*. Saddle Brook, NJ: Fire Engineering Books and Videos, 1997.

Lowe, Joseph D., Jeanne Mesick, Kasey Young, and Mark Huth. *Wildland Firefighting Practices*. Florence, KY: Delmar Publishers, 2000.

Mudd-Ruth, Maria. *Firefighting: Behind the Scenes.* Boston: Houghton Mifflin Co., 1998.

Pyne, Stephen J. *Fire in America: A Cultural History of Wildland and Rural Fire*. Seattle, WA: University of Washington Press, 1997.

Pyne, Stephen J. *Fire on the Rim: A Firefighter's Season at the Grand Canyon*. Seattle, WA: University of Washington Press, 1995.

Teie, William C. *Fire Officer's Handbook on Wildland Firefighting*. Rescue, CA: Deer Valley Press, 1997.

Thoele, Michael. *Fire Line: The Summer Battles of the West*. Golden, CO: Fulcrum Publishing, 1995.

MAGAZINES

Firehouse
Web site: http://server.Firehouse.com

Fire Nuggets
http://www.firenuggets.com

Wildland Firefighter
Web site: http://www.fire-police-ems.com/books/95030.htm

VIDEOS

Wildfire (1994)
Audubon Video.

Wildfires: Fighting Fire with Fire (1995)
A&E. 45 minutes.

Wildland Essentials—Fighting Fire in the Interface (1996)
Wildland Fire Consultants and Seminars.

NATURE PHOTOGRAPHER

Starting out as a nature photographer, all you need is a camera (and it need not be an expensive one), patience, and an artistic eye. Why patience? In the wild, a lot of animals are shy and timid, especially when humans are nearby. Get ready to spend a lot of time out-doors—in the woods, deep in a swamp, on the peak of a mountain, or on the side of a volcano. The really good news is that first those spots are your classroom, and then they are your office. Nice work if you can get it!

Description

The range of career possibilities for a nature photographer is very wide. While not everyone can land a job with *National Geographic* or *Nature* magazine, there are plenty of opportunities for photographers who want to focus their lenses on the natural world. Photographers can earn a living by getting a full-time position at a magazine or other publication, but most nature photographers work on a freelance basis. Freelance work is less steady, but it is a good option for photographers who have built up a reputation or an address book full of clients. Keep your eyes open for opportunities, as they can come from unexpected sources. Businesses, such as outdoor sporting goods and gardening companies, need professional-quality photographers to illustrate their promotional materials (catalogs, Web sites, posters, and other display materials). The greeting card and calendar industries are also possible venues for your images.

Simply stated, a nature photographer must have a love of and respectful appreciation for nature. It is also very important to have a good eye, a visual instinct that allows you to hunt out the most interesting subjects and frame

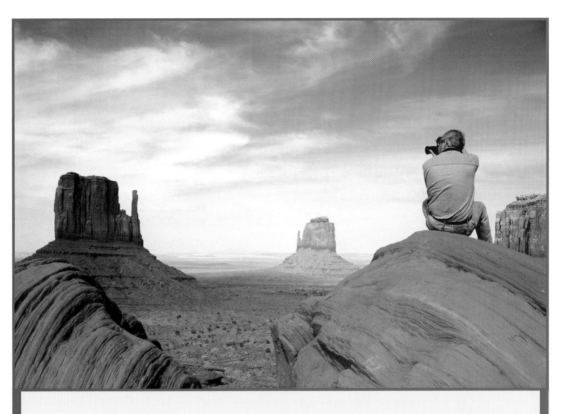

A nature photographer takes shots of Monument Valley in Arizona.

them in the most compelling way. Beyond these essential attributes, the technical aspects of photography can be learned through a combination of formal study (in high school, community college classes, or YMCA workshops) and trial and error.

Nature photography also involves a lot of patience, determination, and an adventurous spirit. You may have to wait for hours for the clouds to clear, for the sun to reach just the right part of the sky, or for an animal to pass before your lens. Sometimes the light will be too harsh or too subdued;

sometimes animals will be partly hidden by trees or grasses or will not stay still for your camera. You will have to learn how to cope with these frustrations and how to compensate for potential limitations. Sometimes only one shot from several rolls of pictures will be worthwhile; you must not let frustration and disappointment prevent you from trying again the next day. Nature photographers must also be adventurous and willing to go to remote and inhospitable places, where the weather may be harsh, in order to take great pictures.

The Nature Photographer's Code of Ethics

- Humans should appear in nature photographs only when they enhance a picture's narrative.
- Pictures of cultivated plants, still-life arrangements, domestic animals, or stuffed and mounted animals are not considered examples of nature photography.
- Photographs manipulated in any way (by computers or airbrushing, for example) are not considered to be true nature photography.
- Do not disturb wild creatures by playing loud music, littering, driving recklessly, or driving off approved roads. If an animal seems agitated, draw back.

- Learn about the behavior of your animal subjects before photographing them. Know when not to interfere with animals' life cycles and respect their routines. Do not approach nests or dens too closely. Never remove fledglings from their nests.
- It is acceptable to remove insects and reptiles from their habitat for photographing, as long as they are returned. Permission to do so from the proper authorities must be granted.
- It is never acceptable to anesthetize an animal for the purposes of nature photography.
- Nocturnal creatures should be photographed in the early morning or late afternoon when they are less active. This will make it easier for you to get the shot, but you will not be disrupting them.
- Cave formations and paintings should never be removed, broken, or tampered with in any way.
- Avoid trampling on grasslands, marshes, and wildflower patches when photographing plants and flowers. Damage to these plants and flowers affects all species in the ecosystem. Stay on designated trails. Wildflowers should never be picked.

Education/Training

Professional nature photographer Ruth Hoyt recommends taking a class, even a general adult education course, as a start. "You can learn on your own, but it's good to get going with some instruction for the technical aspects. Although sometimes it's better to make mistakes and find out later why."

The North American Nature Photography Association sponsors a student scholarship program that is a young photographer's dream come true. Ten high school students are selected annually to attend workshops and trade shows as well as two preliminary days of instructional classes and photo opportunities. Ruth started participating in the program six years ago when she was an aspiring photographer. She says that every year the students put together such a beautiful show that it is just as rewarding for her as it is for them. To be accepted, Ruth says all you need to demonstrate are a love of nature and a keen interest in nature photography.

Outlook

To get started in your new career, spend as much time as possible researching the location and species of everything you photograph. Assign yourself projects, and make every picture a learning opportunity. Ruth says developing your writing skills can definitely set you apart from the pack.

When you feel confident in your skills, go ahead and buy a nature magazine you like and study it, and write to the photo editor for submission guidelines. The rest is up to you. Freelance earnings vary widely, depending on your reputation and experience. Full-time magazine photographers start at about $500 a week and can earn up to $60,000 or more a year (with travel expenses paid) once well established and highly regarded.

Profile

Ruth Hoyt, professional photographer

Ruth Hoyt is an accomplished nature photographer. Her favorite kind of work is shooting close-ups of small details in nature: bugs on leaves, little animals hiding in trees, small birds gliding along the water.

She fell into her career quite by accident. In 1989, her house was broken into and she found herself replacing an expensive camera she had never learned how to use. She signed herself up for a camera class at a local community center and soon discovered a talent she did not know she had. Ruth spent that first summer with a photography group going on field trips. When she entered her first competition the following fall, her photo of a cheetah cub in a hollowed-out log won first place. She had photography fever, and snapping pictures of natural settings became her first love.

It was not long before she decided to quit her day job and devote herself full-time to nature photography. That risky move eventually paid off monetarily and in many other more important ways. Ruth has made her living as a professional nature photographer for ten years now. Her work has appeared in National Geographic publications, a Sierra Club book called Mother Earth, Missouri Magazine of the Columbia Journalism School, and dozens of other publications. Her van has over 300,000 miles on it, which should give you an idea of where her "office" is located. Currently, Ruth directs the Valley Land Fund Wildlife Photo Contest, which entails organizing and conducting the contest, judging the entries, and compiling and publishing the book of winning photos. There is no question that she has followed her heart, and it in turn has rewarded her with this fulfilling career.

Nature photographers work tirelessly to capture beautiful images such as this.

FOR MORE INFORMATION

ASSOCIATIONS

North American Nature Photography Association
Web site: http://www.nanpa.org

Photographic Society of America
Web site: http://www.psa-photo.org

WORKSHOPS

See Apogee's site for more workshops and seminars.

The Nature Workshops
Web site: http://www.natureworkshops.com

Online Photography Seminar
Web site: http://www.photo-seminars.com/index.htm

DISCUSSION GROUP

The Nature.Net Forums
Web site: http://www.nature.net/forums

WEB SITES

ENature.com
http://www.enature.com/guides/select_group.asp
Lets you identify and get information on more than 4,800 birds and animals.

NaturePhotographers.Net Online Magazine
http://www.naturephotographers.net

Valley Land Fund Contest
http://www.valleylandfund.com

Due to the changing nature of Internet links, the Rosen Publishing Group, Inc., has developed an online list of Web sites related to the subject of this book. This site is updated regularly. Please use this link to access the list:

www.rosenlinks.com/ccwc/nalo

MAGAZINES

Apogee Photo
Online photography magazine that often features the special needs of nature photographers.
Web site: http://www.apogeephoto.com

Nature Photographer
P.O. Box 690518
Quincy, MA 02269
(617) 847-0091
Web site: http://www.naturephotographermag.com

Nature Photographers Annual
Web site: http://www.magazania.com/id/cji/group/1494

Popular Photography
1633 Broadway
New York, NY 10019
(212) 767-6000
Web site: http://www.popphoto.com/index.asp

BOOKS

Angel, Heather. *Natural Visions: Creative Tips for Wildlife Photography.* New York: Allworth Press, 2001.

Angel, Heather. *Outdoor Photography: 101 Tips and Hints.* Rochester, NY: Silver Pixel Press, 1998.

Holmes, Judy. *Professional Secrets of Nature Photography: Essential Skills for Photographing Outdoors*. Buffalo, NY: Amherst Media, 2000.

LaPlant, Ralph, and Amy Sharpe. *Outdoor and Survival Skills for Nature Photographers*. Buffalo, NY: Amherst Media, 2000.

Martin, Glen. *National Geographic's Guide to Wildlife Watching: 100 of the Best Places in America to See Animals in Their Natural Habitats*. Washington, DC: National Geographic Society, 1998.

McDonald, Joe. *The New Complete Guide to Wildlife Photography: How to Get Close and Capture Animals on Film*. New York: Watson-Guptill Publications, 1998.

Shaw, John. *John Shaw's Nature Photography Field Guide*. New York: Watson-Guptill Publications, 2000.

Zuckerman, Jim. *Capturing Drama of Nature Photography*. Cincinnati, OH: Writers Digest Books, 2000.

About the Author

Katie Haegele is a freelance writer who lives in Philadelphia.

Photo Credits

Cover © Francois D'elbee/The Image Bank; pp. 9, 10 © Larry Kolvoord/The Image Works; p. 12 © Jacksonville Journal Courier; pp. 20, 24 © Terje Rakke/The Image Bank; p. 23 © Josh Reynolds/The Image Works; pp. 31, 33 © David Hamilton/The Image Bank; p. 34 © Tenton Valley Ranch Camp via The Jackson Hole News, File/AP Wide World Photos; pp. 40, 42, 63, 65 © Michael Doolittle/Peter Arnold, Inc.; p. 44 © Dave Bartruff/Index Stock Imagery, Inc.; pp. 52, 54 © Topham/The Image Works; p. 56 © Jack Fields/Corbis; p. 67 © Syracuse Newspapers/The Image Works; pp. 74, 77 © Victoria Arocho/AP Wide World Photos; p. 79 © Tony Gutierrez/AP Wide World Photos; pp. 84, 86 © Joel W. Rogers/Corbis; p. 88 © Bob Daemmrich/The Image Works; pp. 96, 98 © Peter Pereira/AP Wide World Photos; p. 99 © Stephen Frink/Index Stock Imagery, Inc.; p. 102 © Maritime Safety Agency/AP Wide World Photos; pp. 106, 108 © Karl Weatherly/PhotoDisc; p. 110 © Martin Ruetschi/AP Wide World Photos; pp. 117, 120 © Mike McMillan; p. 118 © James L. Amos/Corbis; pp. 127, 129 © Lynn Eodice/Index Stock Imagery; p. 134 © Digital Stock.

Design and Layout

Evelyn Horovicz